Congratulations!

This is a Bride-to-Be book that captures priceless memories from the exciting first date to the popping of the question: "Will you marry me?"

These are special moments that you and your partner will be able to complete together. This book will be around long after the I Do's when you and your partner want to take a trip down memory lane.

This book alows you to paste pictures, notes, and keepsakes in one place to tell your love story.

We included a section you can use as a diary or extra notes to capture your OMG! to WTF! thoughts.

We hope you have as much fun filling this out as we did.

- Best wishes,

   Ivey and Kyeesha

The Beginning

(name)

(name)

_____

_____

_____

_____

_____

_____

_____

_____

_____

_____

_____

_____

Our Story....
(How we met)

_____

_____

_____

_____

_____

_____

_____

_____

_____

_____

_____

_____

A date to remember...

Date: _____

Place: _____

Date Story: _____

_____

_____

_____

_____

_____

What made this date memorable?

Embarrassing moments
{
- ☐ Food stuck in teeth
- ☐ Wardrobe malfunction
- ☐ Too much to drink
- ☐ "Ex"sposure... oops!
- ☐ Fashionably late

First Impressions

My first impression of _____

_____

_____

_____

_____

_____

_____

_____

_____

_____

_____

_____

_____

First Impressions

My first impression of _____

_____

_____

_____

_____

_____

_____

_____

_____

_____

_____

_____

Your Photo Page!

You're The One...

The moment that I wanted to make _____ my forever was _____

_____

_____

_____

The moment that I wanted to make _____ my forever was _____

_____

_____

_____

Real talk: For us,

☐ Love at first sight

☐ Played hard to get

☐ It's complicated

☐ Other: _____

_____

Omg!
She Proposed

The Proposal

Date: _____

Place: _____

Share the Moment

_____

_____

_____

_____

_____

Emotions

OMG!

I'm so happy...

WTF

Other: _____

_____

_____

_____

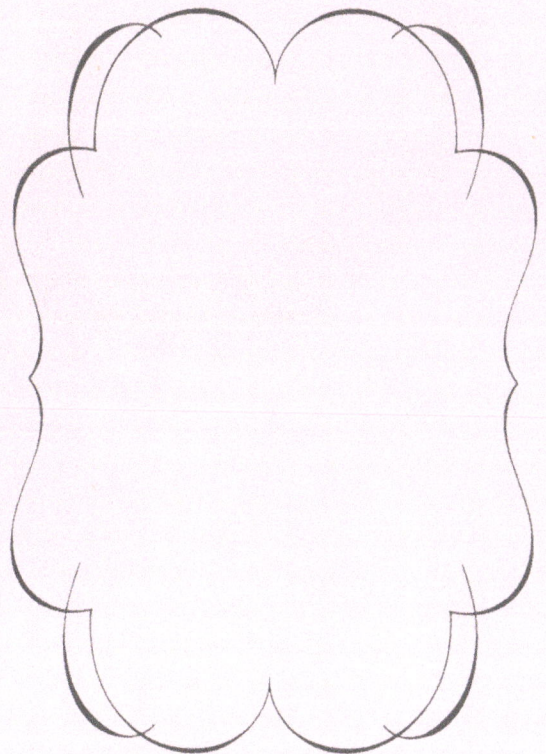

We couldn't wait to tell...

First text sent to: _____

_____

_____

_____

Social media upload: _____

_____

_____

_____

Engagement Photo

Photographed by _____

Date _____

Banded Together

A few words about my engagement ring...

_____

_____

_____

_____

_____

Save the Date

Date of the wedding: _____

Getting To "I Do"

Here's What We're Thinking

Size:

- ☐ Small/Intimate
- ☐ Medium
- ☐ Big & out of control

- ☐ Civil Union
- ☐ Non-Traditional
- ☐ Let's do our own thing!

Style:

- ☐ Casual
- ☐ Traditional
- ☐ Formal

Destination:

- ☐ Church
- ☐ City Hall
- ☐ Vegas baby!

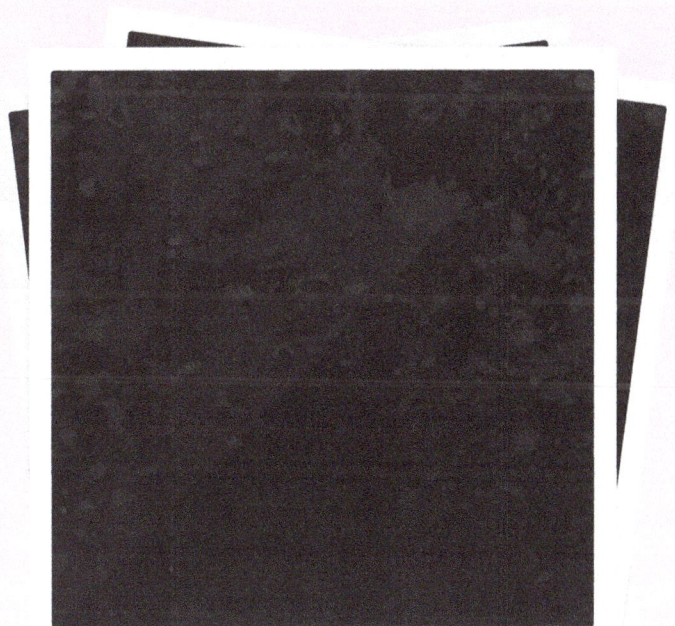

_____ (name)

_____ (name)

_____
_____
_____
_____
_____
_____
_____
_____
_____
_____
_____
_____
_____
_____
_____

Our Wish List

_____
_____
_____
_____
_____
_____
_____
_____
_____
_____
_____
_____
_____
_____
_____

Our Registry

(Where we decided to register or our alternate to registering)

_____

_____

Don't forget to register for:

Kitchen

Bath

Dining & Entertainment

Bedding

Home Appliances

Electronics

Luggage & Travel

Sports & Outdoor

Home Decor

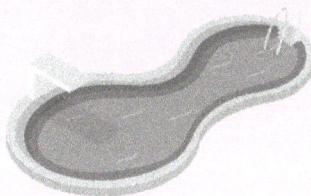

Patio & Garden

Wedding Shower

Here are some people who have shared the love

When: _____

Where: _____

Hosted by: _____

Highlights: _____

_____

_____

Photos

"Almost There!"

The Wedding Party

☐ Just the two of us!

←—— —— ——→   ←—— —— ——→

_____   _____

_____   _____

_____   _____

_____   _____

_____   _____

_____   _____

_____   _____

_____   _____

_____   _____

_____   _____

The Invite

I Said "Yes" to the Dress

I found my dress at _____

It had to have _____

Who helped me pick out my dress _____

_____

_____

My Dress

Traditions
Take 'em or Leave 'em!

"Something" Sentiments

Something Old

_____

_____

Something New

_____

_____

Something Borrowed

_____

_____

Something Blue

_____

_____

Other Sentiments

_____

_____

The Finishing Touches

Details to be remembered

(Hair, make-up, jewelry, etc.)

My Better Half's Attire

Wedding Party Attire

Wedding Party Attire

I vow...

Who's officiating: _____

Influences that we incorporated into the ceremony:

_____

_____

Our vows will be:

☐ Traditional

☐ Wrote Ourselves

☐ "Borrowed" (song lyrics, poem, quotes, etc.)

☐ Other _____

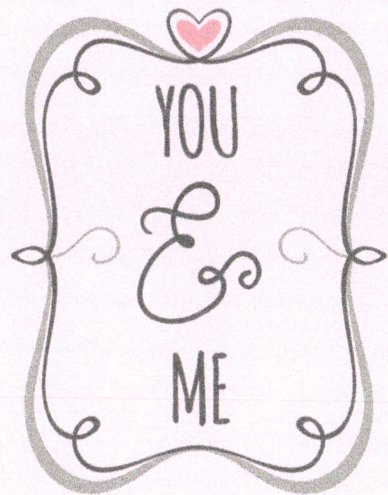

It's Party Time!

We had a Bachlorette Party

- ☐ Joint
- ☐ Seperate
- ☐ Skipped it!

We/ I celebrated on _____

At _____

Details:

_____
_____
_____
_____
_____
_____
_____

We/ I celebrated on _____

At _____

Details:

_____

_____

_____

_____

_____

_____

_____

Our
"I Do"

The Rehearsal

Date: _____

Time: _____

Location: _____

Memorable moments: _____

_____

_____

_____

_____

Photos
(Rehearsal)

Beautiful Petals

Arranged by _____

We chose these flowers because

_____

_____

_____

A Slice of Heaven

Cake made by _____

The flavor(s) _____

Why we chose this cake or alternative

_____

_____

_____

Good Eats

Wedding Menu

_____

_____

_____

_____

_____

_____

_____

_____

Our Wedding Jitters

The first thought when I woke up was _____

_____

_____

_____

The first thought when I woke up was _____

_____

_____

_____

Standing There

My thoughts when I first saw her was _____

_____

_____

_____

My thoughts when I first saw her was _____

_____

_____

_____

Our Wedding Program

Ceremony Photos

The After Party

The Reception

We're married now

Place: _____

Details: _____

_____

_____

_____

Life of the party

Caught the bouquet

_____

Was a dancing queen

_____

Drank the most

_____

Music

Ceremony Music _____

First Dance Song _____

Parent Dance _____

The DJ _____

Our Dance Playlist _____

_____

The First Dance

Options Were

- ☐ Took Lessons
- ☐ Choreographed
- ☐ Not for us!
- ☐ Just go with it!

Photos

Photos

After Thoughts

Aspects of our wedding that went as planned

_____

_____

_____

Surprises along the way

_____

_____

Other

_____

_____

_____

Thoughts from Friends
And Family

The Honeymoon

Love is in the Air

Date: _____

Our Destination: _____
_____

We chose our destination because

_____
_____
_____
_____
_____
_____

Memorable Moments

_____
_____
_____
_____
_____
_____

My Thoughts

A place to vent, my thoughts along this journey

_____

_____

_____

_____

_____

_____

_____

_____

_____

_____

_____

_____

_____

_____

_____

_____

Other books by Ivey and Kyeesha Weaver

Mr & Mr: A Journey from "Will You" to "I Do"

Living as Mrs & Mrs: A Journey After "I Do"

Dating: It's Complicated

Coming Out: A Journey to my Truth